BONNIE AND CLYDE—
THE BEGINNING

BONNIE & CLYDE
THE BEGINNING

Written and drawn by
Gary Jeffrey

LIBRARY OF CONGRESS CATALOGUING-IN-PUBLICATION DATA

Jeffrey, Gary.
Bonnie and Clyde : the beginning /
written and drawn by Gary Jeffrey.
p.   cm.

ISBN 978-0-7864-6540-8
softcover : 50# alkaline paper ∞

1. Parker, Bonnie, 1910–1934—Comic books, strips, etc.   2. Barrow, Clyde, 1909–1934—Comic books, strips, etc.   3. Parker, Bonnie, 1910–1934—Juvenile literature.   4. Barrow, Clyde, 1909–1934—Juvenile literature.   5. Criminals—United States—Biography—Comic books, strips, etc.   6. Criminals—United States—Biography—Juvenile literature.   7. Graphic novels.   I. Title.
HV6245.J37 2014   364.15'52092273—dc23   [B]   2013035468

British Library cataloguing data are available

Cover illustration by Gary Jeffrey

Manufactured in the United States of America

*McFarland & Company, Inc., Publishers
Box 611, Jefferson, North Carolina 28640
www.mcfarlandpub.com*

Police Department

CRIME REPORT

The ordinary folks of America were suffering hard through the early years of the Great Depression...

...but obviously people still had to make a living...

3

5

7

9

CLICK

12

WHAT IS IT THEY SAY?

THE BEST LAID PLANS?...

...WELL CLYDE BOY, YOUR GRAND PLANS ARE JUST ABOUT **SHOT**.

...THANKS TO **RUSSELL** AND **RODGERS** THERE.

WHEN I THINK BACK TO WHERE I CAME FROM...

...CROSSING THE DIRTY TRINITY FOR THE FIRST TIME...

...INTO THE CITY.

15

21

GREETINGS FROM WITCHITA

-WITCHITA FALLS?

-BONNIE!

PLACE STAMP HERE

POST CARD

Dearest Mother,
This is just a note to let
you know that I am fine
I got the job in the cafe and
I rented a nice little
apartment for myself. It has
a sofa and a small kitchen
where I can cook simple meals
I miss you mama and I will
come home as soon as I am able.
but I know that this is for
the best—a fresh start—away
from Dallas—away from 'trouble'
all my love—your Bonnie

24

25

31

...approaching the outskirts of West Dallas the perpetrators were observed by two off-duty sheriffs who commenced to give chase to the stolen Ford...

JESUS!

VAROOOOOOO

WHERE THE **HELL'S** HE GOING IN SUCH A **HURRY?**

DON'T KNOW —BUT WE'LL SOON FIND OUT!

...had to reluctantly give up the high speed chase due to being out-distanced by the more powerful Ford...

YOU SEE *CLYDE*...

Grand Prairie, Texas

The "One Way Wagon", Mclennan County Jail, Waco, Texas, September 18, 1930

40

*BONNIE'S PETTY CRIMINAL FIRST HUSBAND

43

44

47

51

McKinney Bus Terminal, Texas

?!

YOU'VE BEEN MIGHTY *CO-OPERATIVE* ROSS*, I MUST SAY.

AREN'T YOU *'FRAID* YOUR FRIENDS'LL COME BACK AN' *FIND YOU*, SEEIN' AS HOW YOU *FINGERED* 'EM AND ALL?

NAH. I'LL BE AWAY FOR A GOOD WHILE —RIGHT?

BESIDES, THE BOYS *TOLD ME* —THEY AIN'T GONNA BE TAKEN *ALIVE*.

54

*ROSS DYER—EVERETT MULLIGAN'S ALIAS

CARLSBAD, NEW MEXICO
August 15

HMMMM...

...THAT COUPE'S GOT TEXAS PLATES...

...THINK I'LL MAKE A NOTE OF THAT NUMBER...

NOW, I WANT YOU BOYS TO BE ON YOUR BEST BEHAVOIR MY AUNT'S A RESPECTABLE LADY...

...GET IT CHECKED OUT...

THIS HERE'S MY HUSBAND "JOHN" AN' WE BROUGHT A FRIEND...

PLEASED TO MEET YOU MRS. STAMPS.

CALL ME NETTIE...

KNOCK KNOCK

SHIT! NEED A GUN, NEED A GUN!

OURS ARE LOCKED IN THE *TRUNK* —MUST BE ONE IN THE *HOUSE?*

MORNIN' MISS, I'D LIKE TO TALK TO THE OWNER OF THE CAR *OUT FRONT.*

THE ONE WITH *TEXAS* PLATES?

GOT IT!

WHY SURE, OFFICER. IT BELONGS TO A FRIEND OF MINE WHO IS VISITING.

HE'S JUST *DRESSING* AND WILL BE OUT IN A FEW *MINUTES.*

59

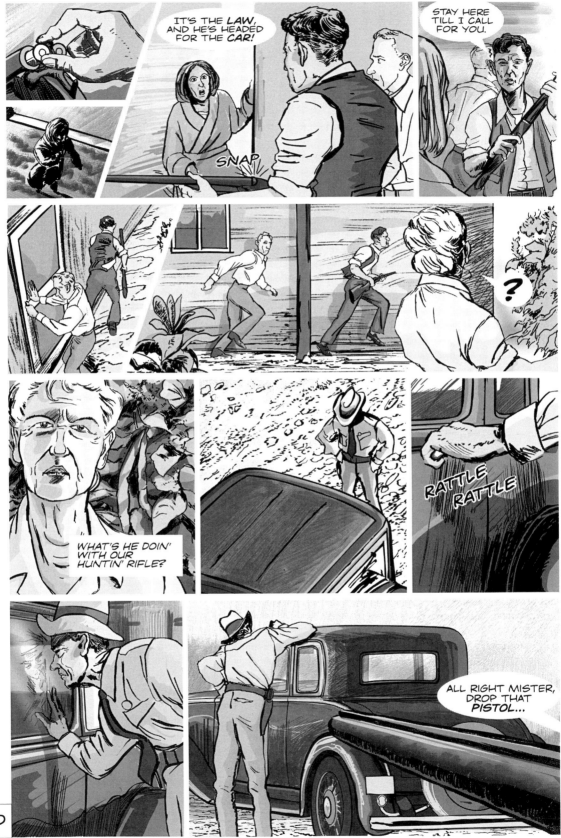

67

Michigan, September

75

JESUS—SHIT!!

OLE CLYDE SURE PLAYS *HARD TO GET* DON'T HE?

I'M JUS' *GLAD* IT AIN'T *ME.*

I'M SURE CLYDE'LL *ENJOY* HIS *RIDE* THO'...

HEH HEH HEH

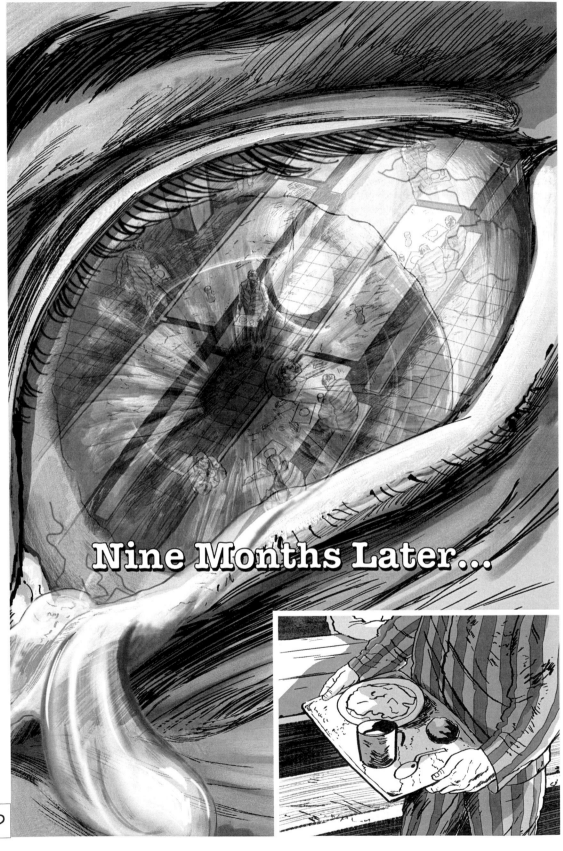

Nine Months Later...

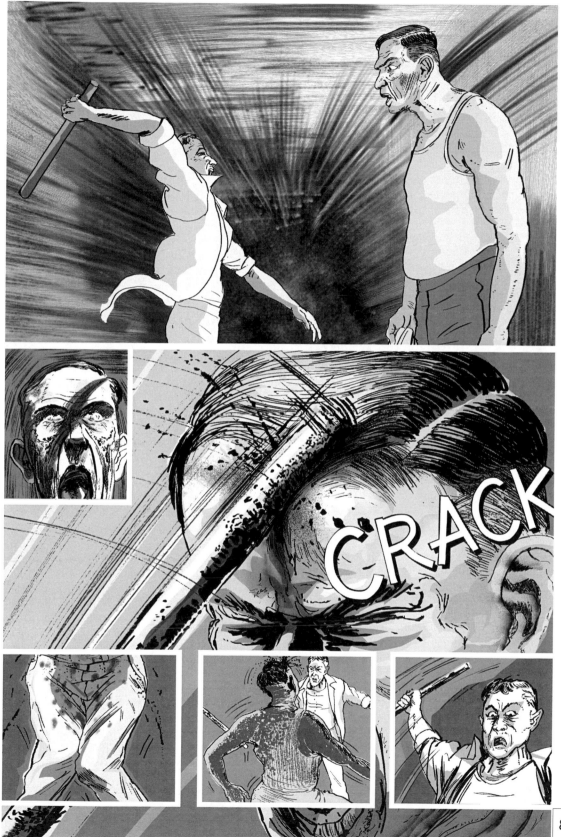

CRACK

89

FIGHT! FIGHT!

SCALLEY AN' CROWDER ARE HAVING A KNIFE FIGHT!

BLAM

103

119

TEMPLE, TEXAS, December 25

123

129

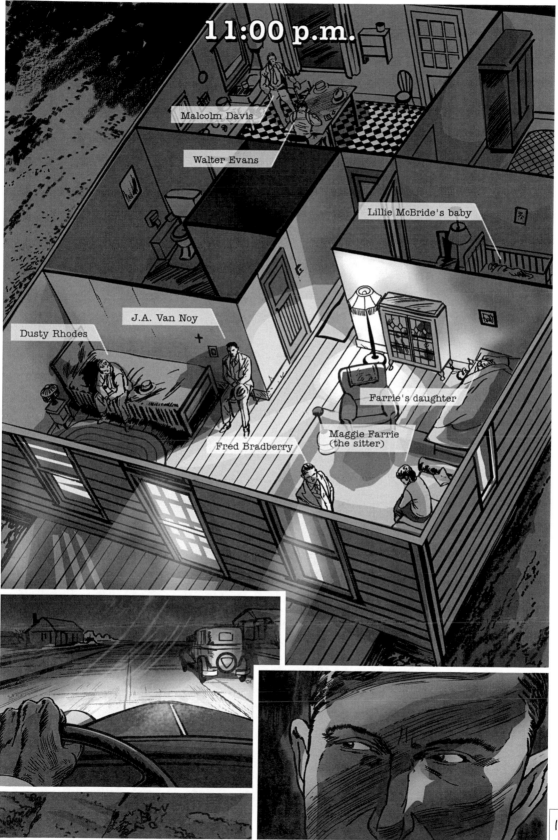

145

147

GOD...

...I'M *SORRY* ABOUT *LON*, SHERIFF.

SON OF A *BITCH*...

...WHO THE *HELL* WAS THAT—IT DIDN'T LOOK LIKE *CHAMBLESS* TO ME!

IT *WEREN'T* CHAMBLESS...

IT WAS SOMEONE CALLED *CLYDE BARROW*...

153

The Caldwell Farm, Wilmer, Texas

169

183

199

202

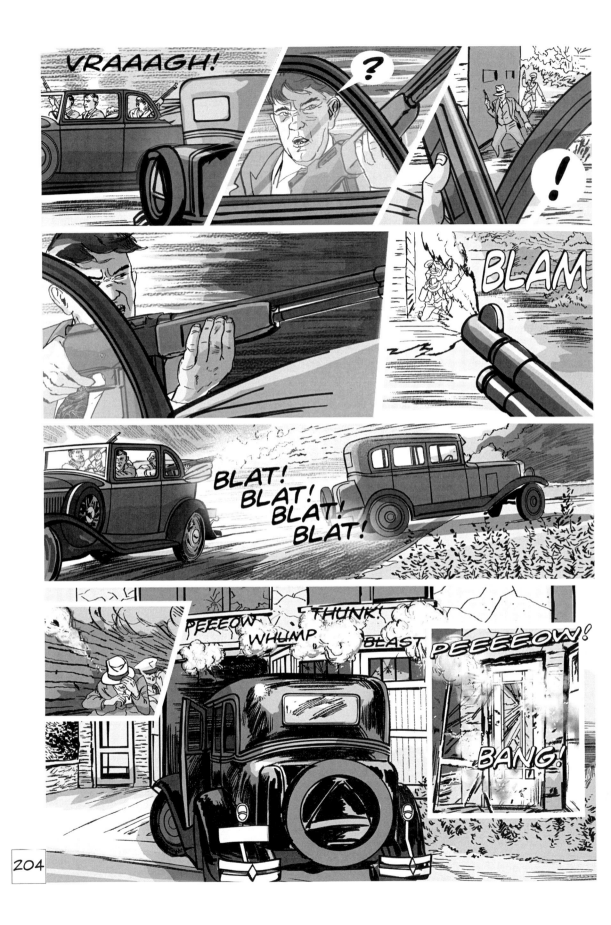

...FANCY CLOTHES, AN *ARSENAL*—WHOEVER THEY WERE THEY WEREN'T *BOOTLEGGERS*.

ARMED TO THE *TEETH*—HARRY NEVER *STOOD A CHANCE*...

CAPTAIN POTLEY, I FOUND A *PURSE*.

WHAT'S THIS?

A MARRIAGE LICENSE "BLANCHE CALDWELL".

AND HERE—A PARDON FROM THE *TEXAS* STATE GOVERNOR...

...MADE OUT TO HER *HUSBAND*.

CITY of JOPLIN
POLICE PATROL DIVISION
JOPLIN MISSOURI

IDENTIFICATION
ORDER NO. 1201

BULLETIN ISSUED:
APRIL 25, 1933

WANTED

FUGITIVES

CLYDE BARROW

FROM

BONNIE PARKER

JUSTICE

FUGITIVE **MURDER** WARRANTS HAVE BEEN ISSUED FOR CLYDE CHAMPION BARROW & BONNIE PARKER. IN A SHOOT OUT WITH LOCAL AUTHORITIES IN JOPLIN, MO., ON APRIL 13, 1933, CLYDE BARROW IS KNOWN TO HAVE KILLED DETECTIVE HARRY McGINNIS & CONSTABLE J.W. HARRYMAN. OTHER MEMBERS OF THE BARROW GANG IN THE GUN BATTLE WERE CLYDE'S OLDER BROTHER MARVIN "BUCK" BARROW & W.D. "DEACON" JONES, A HOMETOWN FRIEND & ASSOCIATE. ALSO PRESENT WITH THE GANG IN A TWO STOREY APARTMENT HOUSE THEY HAD SUBLET UNDER AN ASSUMED NAME WAS "BUCK'S" WIFE, BLANCHE BARROW. SHE IS BEING SOUGHT AS A MATERIAL WITNESS. ALL MEMBERS OF THE BARROW GANG ARE KNOWN TO BE HEAVILY ARMED AT ALL TIMES & EXTREMELY DANGEROUS.

FUGITIVES

CLYDE BARROW

FROM

BONNIE PARKER

JUSTICE

213

ACKNOWLEDGEMENTS

THANKS TO:

Peter Richardson, UK illustrator, for unsolicited initial encouragement

Colleague Frederique Etienney for her interest & enthusiasm

Friend James Lappin for being an early reader

Neighbor and friend Tim Hawkins for telling me to send it out

Old friend and college chum Richard Jones for *unbridled* enthusiasm

Main employer David West for giving me years of "practise"

Editor Natalie Foreman for being willing to take a punt

And finally...Lynne, Charlie and Harvey for going through the "ordeal" of
making this book alongside me without (too much) complaint

BIBLIOGRAPHY

*The True Story of Bonnie & Clyde: As Told by Bonnie's Mother [Emma Parker]
and Clyde's Sister [Nell Barrow Cowan]*
Emma Krause Parker, Nellie (Barrow) Cowan—New American Library 1968

The Lives and Times of Bonnie and Clyde
E. R. Milner—SIU Press 2003

Go Down Together: The True, Untold Story of Bonnie and Clyde
Jeff Guinn—Simon and Schuster 2009

My Life with Bonnie and Clyde
Blanche Caldwell Barrow—University of Oklahoma Press 2012

And the excellent website:
http://texashideout.tripod.com/bc.htm

McFarland Graphic Novels

Yellow Rose of Texas: The Myth of Emily Morgan.
Written by Douglas Brode; Illustrated by Joe Orsak. 2010

Horrors: Great Stories of Fear and Their Creators.
Written by Rocky Wood; Illustrated by Glenn Chadbourne. 2010

Hutch: Baseball's Fred Hutchinson and a Legacy of Courage.
Written by Mike Shannon; Illustrated by Scott Hannig. 2011

*Hit by Pitch: Ray Chapman, Carl Mays and
the Fatal Fastball.* Molly Lawless. 2012

*Werewolves of Wisconsin and Other American Myths,
Monsters and Ghosts.* Andy Fish. 2012

Witch Hunts: A Graphic History of the Burning Times.
Written by Rocky Wood and Lisa Morton;
Illustrated by Greg Chapman. 2012

*Hardball Legends and Journeymen and Short-Timers: 333
Illustrated Baseball Biographies.* Ronnie Joyner. 2012

The Accidental Candidate: The Rise and Fall of Alvin Greene.
Written by Corey Hutchins and David Axe; Art by Blue Delliquanti. 2012

Virgin Vampires: Or, Once Upon a Time in Transylvania.
Written by Douglas Brode; Illustrated by Joe Orsak. 2012

Great Zombies in History.
Edited by Joe Sergi. 2013